ELIZABETH II

Protection of Badgers Act 1992

1992 CHAPTER 51

An Act to consolidate the Badgers Act 1973, the Badgers Act 1991 and the Badgers (Further Protection) Act 1991. [16th July 1992]

B E IT ENACTED by the Queen's most Excellent Majesty, by and with the advice and consent of the Lords Spiritual and Temporal, and Commons, in this present Parliament assembled, and by the authority of the same, as follows:—

Offences

1.—(1) A person is guilty of an offence if, except as permitted by or under this Act, he wilfully kills, injures or takes, or attempts to kill, injure or take, a badger.

Taking, injuring or killing badgers.

(2) If, in any proceedings for an offence under subsection (1) above consisting of attempting to kill, injure or take a badger, there is evidence from which it could reasonably be concluded that at the material time the accused was attempting to kill, injure or take a badger, he shall be presumed to have been attempting to kill, injure or take a badger unless the contrary is shown.

(3) A person is guilty of an offence if, except as permitted by or under this Act, he has in his possession or under his control any dead badger or any part of, or anything derived from, a dead badger.

(4) A person is not guilty of an offence under subsection (3) above if he shows that—

    (a) the badger had not been killed, or had been killed otherwise than in contravention of the provisions of this Act or of the Badgers Act 1973; or

1973 c. 57.

    (b) the badger or other thing in his possession or control had been sold (whether to him or any other person) and, at the time of the purchase, the purchaser had had no reason to believe that the badger had been killed in contravention of any of those provisions.

(5) If a person is found committing an offence under this section on any land it shall be lawful for the owner or occupier of the land, or any servant of the owner or occupier, or any constable, to require that person forthwith to quit the land and also to give his name and address; and if that person on being so required wilfully remains on the land or refuses to give his full name or address he is guilty of an offence.

Cruelty.

2.—(1) A person is guilty of an offence if—

    (a) he cruelly ill-treats a badger;

    (b) he uses any badger tongs in the course of killing or taking, or attempting to kill or take, a badger;

    (c) except as permitted by or under this Act, he digs for a badger; or

    (d) he uses for the purpose of killing or taking a badger any firearm other than a smooth bore weapon of not less than 20 bore or a rifle using ammunition having a muzzle energy not less than 160 footpounds and a bullet weighing not less than 38 grains.

(2) If in any proceedings for an offence under subsection (1)(c) above there is evidence from which it could reasonably be concluded that at the material time the accused was digging for a badger he shall be presumed to have been digging for a badger unless the contrary is shown.

Interfering with badger setts.

3. A person is guilty of an offence if, except as permitted by or under this Act, he interferes with a badger sett by doing any of the following things—

    (a) damaging a badger sett or any part of it;

    (b) destroying a badger sett;

    (c) obstructing access to, or any entrance of, a badger sett;

    (d) causing a dog to enter a badger sett; or

    (e) disturbing a badger when it is occupying a badger sett,

intending to do any of those things or being reckless as to whether his actions would have any of those consequences.

Selling and possession of live badgers.

4. A person is guilty of an offence if, except as permitted by or under this Act, he sells a live badger or offers one for sale or has a live badger in his possession or under his control.

Marking and ringing.

5. A person is guilty of an offence if, except as authorised by a licence under section 10 below, he marks, or attaches any ring, tag or other marking device to, a badger other than one which is lawfully in his possession by virtue of such a licence.

Exceptions and licences

General exceptions.

6. A person is not guilty of an offence under this Act by reason only of—

    (a) taking or attempting to take a badger which has been disabled otherwise than by his act and is taken or to be taken solely for the purpose of tending it;

    (b) killing or attempting to kill a badger which appears to be so seriously injured or in such a condition that to kill it would be an act of mercy;

(c) unavoidably killing or injuring a badger as an incidental result of a lawful action;

(d) doing anything which is authorised under the Animals (Scientific Procedures) Act 1986.   1986 c. 14.

7.—(1) Subject to subsection (2) below, a person is not guilty of an offence under section 1(1) above by reason of—   Exceptions from s. 1.

(a) killing or taking, or attempting to kill or take, a badger; or

(b) injuring a badger in the course of taking it or attempting to kill or take it,

if he shows that his action was necessary for the purpose of preventing serious damage to land, crops, poultry or any other form of property.

(2) The defence provided by subsection (1) above does not apply in relation to any action taken at any time if it had become apparent, before that time, that the action would prove necessary for the purpose there mentioned and either—

(a) a licence under section 10 below authorising that action had not been applied for as soon as reasonably practicable after that fact had become apparent; or

(b) an application for such a licence had been determined.

8.—(1) Subject to subsection (2) below, a person is not guilty of an offence under section 3 above if he shows that his action was necessary for the purpose of preventing serious damage to land, crops, poultry or any other form of property.   Exceptions from s. 3.

(2) Subsection (2) of section 7 above applies to the defence in subsection (1) above as it applies to the defence in subsection (1) of that section.

(3) A person is not guilty of an offence under section 3(a), (c) or (e) above if he shows that his action was the incidental result of a lawful operation and could not reasonably have been avoided.

(4) A person is not guilty of an offence under section 3(a), (c) or (e) above by reason of obstructing any entrance of a badger sett for the purpose of hunting foxes with hounds if he—

(a) takes no action other than obstructing such entrances;

(b) does not dig into the tops or sides of the entrances;

(c) complies with subsection (5) below as to the materials used for obstructing the entrances and with subsection (6) below as to how and when they are to be placed and removed; and

(d) is acting with the authority of the owner or occupier of the land and the authority of a recognised Hunt.

(5) The materials used shall be only—

(a) untainted straw or hay, or leaf-litter, bracken or loose soil; or

(b) a bundle of sticks or faggots, or paper sacks either empty or filled with untainted straw or hay or leaf-litter, bracken or loose soil.

(6) The materials shall not be packed hard into the entrances and—

    (a) if they are of the kind mentioned in paragraph (a) of subsection (5) above, they shall not be placed in the entrances except on the day of the hunt or after midday on the preceding day;

    (b) if they are of the kind mentioned in paragraph (b) of that subsection, they shall not be placed in the entrances except on the day of the hunt and shall be removed on the same day.

(7) A person is not guilty of an offence under section 3(a), (c) or (e) above by reason of his hounds marking at a badger sett provided they are withdrawn as soon as reasonably practicable.

(8) Each recognised Hunt shall keep a register of the persons authorised to act under subsection (4) above.

(9) In this section "recognised Hunt" means a Hunt recognised by the Masters of Fox Hounds Association, the Association of Masters of Harriers and Beagles or the Central Committee of Fell Packs.

Exceptions from s. 4.

9. A person is not guilty of an offence under section 4 above by reason of having a live badger in his possession or under his control if—

    (a) it is in his possession or under his control, as the case may be, in the course of his business as a carrier; or

    (b) it has been disabled otherwise than by his act and taken by him solely for the purpose of tending it and it is necessary for that purpose for it to remain in his possession or under his control, as the case may be.

Licences.

10.—(1) A licence may be granted to any person by the appropriate Conservancy Council authorising him, notwithstanding anything in the foregoing provisions of this Act, but subject to compliance with any conditions specified in the licence—

    (a) for scientific or educational purposes or for the conservation of badgers—

        (i) to kill or take, within an area specified in the licence by any means so specified, or to sell, or to have in his possession, any number of badgers so specified; or

        (ii) to interfere with any badger sett within an area specified in the licence by any means so specified;

    (b) for the purpose of any zoological gardens or collection specified in the licence, to take within an area specified in the licence by any means so specified, or to sell, or to have in his possession, any number of badgers so specified;

    (c) for the purpose of ringing and marking, to take badgers within an area specified in the licence, to mark such badgers or to attach to them any ring, tag or other marking device as specified in the licence;

    (d) for the purpose of any development as defined in section 55(1) of the Town and Country Planning Act 1990 or, as respects Scotland, section 19(1) of the Town and Country Planning (Scotland) Act 1972, to interfere with a badger sett within an area specified in the licence by any means so specified;

1990 c. 8.
1972 c. 52.

(e) for the purpose of the preservation, or archaeological investigation, of a monument scheduled under section 1 of the Ancient Monuments and Archaeological Areas Act 1979, to interfere with a badger sett within an area specified in the licence by any means so specified;   1979 c. 46.

(f) for the purpose of investigating whether any offence has been committed or gathering evidence in connection with proceedings before any court, to interfere with a badger sett within an area specified in the licence by any means so specified.

(2) A licence may be granted to any person by the appropriate Minister authorising him, notwithstanding anything in the foregoing provisions of this Act, but subject to compliance with any conditions specified in the licence—

(a) for the purpose of preventing the spread of disease, to kill or take badgers, or to interfere with a badger sett, within an area specified in the licence by any means so specified;

(b) for the purpose of preventing serious damage to land, crops, poultry or any other form of property, to kill or take badgers, or to interfere with a badger sett, within an area specified in the licence by any means so specified;

(c) for the purpose of any agricultural or forestry operation, to interfere with a badger sett within an area specified in the licence by any means so specified;

(d) for the purpose of any operation (whether by virtue of the Land Drainage Act 1991 or otherwise) to maintain or improve any existing watercourse or drainage works, or to construct new works required for the drainage of any land, including works for the purpose of defence against sea water or tidal water, to interfere with a badger sett within an area specified in the licence by any means so specified.   1991 c. 59.

(3) A licence may be granted to any person either by the appropriate Conservancy Council or the appropriate Minister authorising that person, notwithstanding anything in the foregoing provisions of this Act, but subject to compliance with any conditions specified in the licence, to interfere with a badger sett within an area specified in the licence by any means so specified for the purpose of controlling foxes in order to protect livestock, game or wild life.

(4) In this section "the appropriate Conservancy Council" means, in relation to a licence for an area—

(a) in England, the Nature Conservancy Council for England;

(b) in Wales, the Countryside Council for Wales; and

(c) in Scotland, Scottish Natural Heritage.

(5) In this section "the appropriate Minister" means in relation to a licence for an area—

(a) in England, the Minister of Agriculture, Fisheries and Food; and

(b) in Wales or in Scotland, the Secretary of State.

(6) The appropriate Minister shall from time to time consult with the appropriate Conservancy Council as to the exercise of his functions under subsection (2)(b), (c) or (d) above and shall not grant a licence of any description unless he has been advised by the appropriate Conservancy Council as to the circumstances in which, in that Council's opinion, licences of that description should be granted.

(7) In relation to Scottish Natural Heritage subsection (6) above shall have effect with the omission of the reference to subsection (2)(c) and (d).

(8) A licence granted under this section may be revoked at any time by the authority by whom it was granted, and without prejudice to any other liability to a penalty which he may have incurred under this or any other Act, a person who contravenes or fails to comply with any condition imposed on the grant of a licence under this section is guilty of an offence.

(9) A licence under this section shall not be unreasonably withheld or revoked.

(10) It shall be a defence in proceedings for an offence under section 8(b) of the Protection of Animals Act 1911 or section 7(b) of the Protection of Animals (Scotland) Act 1912 (each of which restricts the placing on land of poison and poisonous substances) to show that—

1911 c. 27.
1912 c. 14.

(a) the act alleged to constitute the offence was done under the authority of a licence granted under subsection (2)(a) above; and

(b) any conditions specified in the licence were complied with.

Enforcement and penalties

Powers of constables.

1973 c. 57.

11. Where a constable has reasonable grounds for suspecting that a person is committing an offence under the foregoing provisions of this Act, or has committed an offence under those provisions or those of the Badgers Act 1973 and that evidence of the commission of the offence is to be found on that person or any vehicle or article he may have with him, the constable may—

(a) without warrant stop and search that person and any vehicle or article he may have with him;

(b) seize and detain for the purposes of proceedings under any of those provisions anything which may be evidence of the commission of the offence or may be liable to be forfeited under section 12(4) below;

(c) in Scotland arrest that person without warrant if he fails to give his full name and address to the constable's satisfaction.

Penalties and forfeiture.

12.—(1) A person guilty of an offence under section 1(1) or (3), 2 or 3 above is liable on summary conviction to imprisonment for a term not exceeding six months or a fine not exceeding level 5 on the standard scale or both; and a person guilty of an offence under section 4, 5 or 10(8) above or 13(7) below is liable on summary conviction to a fine not exceeding that level.

(2) Where an offence was committed in respect of more than one badger the maximum fine which may be imposed under subsection (1) above shall be determined as if the person convicted had been convicted of a separate offence in respect of each badger.

(3) A person guilty of an offence under section 1(5) above is liable on summary conviction to a fine not exceeding level 3 on the standard scale.

(4) The court by which a person is convicted of an offence under this Act shall order the forfeiture of any badger or badger skin in respect of which the offence was committed and may, if they think fit, order the forfeiture of any weapon or article in respect of or by means of which the offence was committed.

13.—(1) Where a dog has been used in or was present at the commission of an offence under sections 1(1), 2 or 3 above, the court, on convicting the offender, may, in addition to or in substitution for any other punishment, make either or both of the following orders—

Powers of court where dog used or present at commission of offence.

    (a) an order for the destruction or other disposal of the dog;

    (b) an order disqualifying the offender, for such period as it thinks fit, for having custody of a dog.

(2) Where the court makes an order under subsection (1)(a) above, it may—

    (a) appoint a person to undertake the destruction or other disposal of the dog and require any person having custody of the dog to deliver it up for that purpose; and

    (b) order the offender to pay such sum as the court may determine to be the reasonable expenses of destroying or otherwise disposing of the dog and of keeping it pending its destruction or disposal.

(3) Where an order under subsection (1)(a) above is made in relation to a dog owned by a person other than the offender, the owner of the dog may appeal to the Crown Court against the order.

(4) A dog shall not be destroyed pursuant to an order under subsection (1)(a) above—

    (a) until the end of the period within which notice of appeal to the Crown Court against the order can be given; and

    (b) if notice of appeal is given in that period, until the appeal is determined or withdrawn,

unless the owner of the dog gives notice to the court which made the order that he does not intend to appeal against it.

(5) A person who is disqualified for having custody of a dog by virtue of an order made under subsection (1)(b) above may, at any time after the end of the period of one year beginning with the date of the order, apply to the court that made it (or any magistrates' court acting for the same petty sessions area as that court) for a direction terminating the disqualification.

(6) On an application under subsection (5) above the court may—

    (a) having regard to the applicant's character, his conduct since the disqualification was imposed and any other circumstances of the case, grant or refuse the application; and

(b) order the applicant to pay all or any part of the costs of the application;

and where an application in respect of an order is refused no further application in respect of that order shall be entertained if made before the end of the period of one year beginning with the date of the refusal.

(7) Any person who—

(a) has custody of a dog in contravention of an order under subsection (1)(b) above; or

(b) fails to comply with a requirement imposed on him under subsection (2)(a) above,

is guilty of an offence.

(8) A sum ordered to be paid by an order under subsection (2)(b) above shall be recoverable summarily as a civil debt.

(9) In the application of this section to Scotland—

(a) in subsection (3), for the words "Crown Court against the order" there shall be substituted the words "High Court of Justiciary against the order within the period of seven days beginning with the date of the order";

(b) for subsection (4)(a) there shall be substituted—

"(a) until the end of the period of seven days beginning with the date of the order"; and

(c) in subsection (5), the words "(or any magistrates' court acting for the same petty sessions area as that court)" shall be omitted.

Interpretation.

1968 c. 27.

14. In this Act—

"ammunition" has the same meaning as in the Firearms Act 1968;

"badger" means any animal of the species *Meles meles*;

"badger sett" means any structure or place which displays signs indicating current use by a badger;

"firearm" has the same meaning as in the Firearms Act 1968;

"sale" includes hire, barter and exchange and cognate expressions shall be construed accordingly.

Short title, repeals, commencement and extent.

15.—(1) This Act may be cited as the Protection of Badgers Act 1992.

(2) The enactments mentioned in the Schedule to this Act are repealed to the extent specified in the third column of that Schedule.

(3) This Act shall come into force at the end of the period of three months beginning with the day on which it is passed.

(4) This Act does not extend to Northern Ireland.

SCHEDULE

REPEALS

Chapter	Short title	Extent of repeal
1973 c. 57.	The Badgers Act 1973.	The whole Act.
1981 c. 69.	The Wildlife and Countryside Act 1981.	Section 73(4). In Schedule 7, paragraphs 8 to 12.
1985 c. 31.	The Wildlife and Countryside (Amendment) Act 1985.	Section 1.
1986 c. 14.	The Animals (Scientific Procedures) Act 1986.	In Schedule 3, paragraph 9.
1990 c. 43.	The Environmental Protection Act 1990.	In Schedule 9, paragraph 6.
1991 c. 28.	The Natural Heritage (Scotland) Act 1991.	In Schedule 2, paragraph 5.
1991 c. 35.	The Badgers (Further Protection) Act 1991.	The whole Act.
1991 c. 36.	The Badgers Act 1991.	The whole Act.
1991 c. 53.	The Criminal Justice Act 1991.	Section 26(3).

TABLE OF DERIVATIONS

Note:

The following abbreviations are used in this Table:—

1973	= The Badgers Act 1973 (c.57)
1975	= The Conservation of Wild Creatures and Wild Plants Act 1975 (c.48)
1981	= The Wildlife and Countryside Act 1981 (c.69)
1985	= The Wildlife and Countryside (Amendment) Act 1985 (c.31)
1986	= The Animals (Scientific Procedures) Act 1986 (c.14)
1990	= The Environmental Protection Act 1990 (c.43)
1991 (S)	= The Natural Heritage (Scotland) Act 1991 (c.28)
1991 (FP)	= The Badgers (Further Protection) Act 1991 (1991 c.35)
1991	= The Badgers Act 1991 (1991 c.36)

Section of Act	Derivation
1(1)	1973 s.1(1); 1985 s.1(1)(a)
(2)	1973 s.1(1A); 1985 s.1(1)(b)
(3)	1973 s.1(2); 1981, Sch.7, para 8
(4)	1973 s.1(3); 1981, Sch.7, para 8
(5)	1973 s.5
2(1)	1973 s.2(1); 1981, Sch.7, para 9(2); 1985 s.1(2)(a)
(2)	1973 s.2(2); 1985 s.1(2)(b)
3	1973 s.2(3); 1991 s.1
4	1973 s.3
5	1973 s.4
6	1973 s.8(1), (3); 1986, Sch.3, para 9
7	1973 s.8(1A), (1B); 1981, Sch.7, para 10(1)
8(1), (2)	1973 s.8(1A), (1B); 1981, Sch.7, para 10(1); 1991 s.2(1)
(3)	1973 s.8(4); 1991 s.2(2)
(4) to (9)	1973 s.8(5), (6); 1991 s.3
9	1973 s.8(2) (s.8(2)(a) spent); s.8(2)(c) rep. 1981, Sch.7, para 9(4), Sch.17, Part II)
10(1)(a)	1973 s.9(1)(a), (2)(a); 1991 s.4(a); 1991(S) Sch.2, para.5(2)
(b)	1973 s.9(1)(b), (2)(a)

Section of Act	Derivation
(c)	1973 s.9(1)(c), (2)(a)
(d)	1973 s.9(1)(f), (2)(a); 1991 s.4 (d), (e)
(e)	1973 s.9(1)(j), (2)(a); 1991 s.4(d), (e)
(f)	1973 s.9(1)(i), (2)(a); 1991 s.4(d), (e)
(2)(a)	1973 s.9(1)(d), (2)(b); 1991 s.4(b)
(b)	1973 s.9(1)(e), (2)(b); 1981, Sch.7, para 10(2), (3); 1991 s.4(c)
(c)	1973 s.9(1)(g), (2)(b); 1991 s.4(d), (f)
(d)	1973 s.9(1)(h), (2)(b); 1991 s.4(d), (f)
(3)	1973 s.9(1)(k), (2)(c); 1991 s.4(d), (g)
(4)	1973 s.9(2)(a); 1990, Sch.9, para 6(2); 1991(S), Sch.2, para 5(2)
(5)	1973 s.9(2)(b); The Transfer of Functions (Wales) (No.1) Order 1978 (S.I. 1978/272)
(6), (7)	1973 s.9(4),(4A); 1981, Sch.7, para 10(4); 1990, Sch.9, para 6(3); 1991(S), Sch.2, para 5(3); 1991 s.4(h)
(8)	1973 s.9(3)
(9)	1973 s.9(6); 1991 s.4(i)
(10)	1973 s.9(4); 1975 s.16 (saved by 1981 s.73(4))
11	1973 s.10(1); 1981, Sch.7, para 11(1) (s.10(1)(b) repealed (E&W) by Police and Criminal Evidence Act 1984 (c.60), Sch.7, Part I)
12(1), (2), (3)	1973 s.10(2); 1981, Sch.7, para 11(2); Criminal Justice Act 1982 (c.48) s.46; Criminal Procedure (Scotland) Act 1975 (c.21) s.289G; Criminal Justice Act 1991 s.26(3); S.I. 1991/2208 art 2(3); S.I. 1991/2706 art.2(2); 1991(FP) s.1(7)
(4)	1973 s.10(3)
13	1991 (FP) s.1
14	1973 s.11; 1981, Sch.7, para 12; 1991 s.5
15(1)	—
(2)	—
(3)	—
(4)	1973 s.12(2); 1991 (FP) s.2(4)

Printed in the UK for The Stationery Office Limited
under the authority and superintendence of Carol Tullo, Controller of
Her Majesty's Stationery Office and Queen's Printer of Acts of Parliament.

Dd759846   10/97   1731/2   19585   Job No. JOO050

1st Impression July 1992
3rd Impression October 1997